The Complete Medical Bill Translator

This charge may vary.

By Jordan K. Ledger, M.B.A.

This work is satire. No medical, legal, or billing advice is provided.

ISBN: 9798276103990

Edited, printed and laughed with in the USA.

"Pricing subject to change without notice."

—Anonymous Administrator

For anyone who has ever opened a bill and whispered, "What?"

Table of Contents

Preface: A Formality

Medical billing is complex, adaptive, and occasionally hostile.

This handbook seeks to clarify almost nothing. Any resemblance to useful guidance is accidental and should be corrected immediately.

Chapter 1 – Introduction to Variable Billing

Charges in healthcare drift like weather systems—unpredictable, unmoved by reason, and largely immune to inquiry.

Term: Charge Adjustment

Translation: We changed it.

Term: Facility Fee

Translation: Existing fees lacked ambition.

Term: Clarification Request

Translation: Misfiled immediately.

Term: Level-2 Processing

Translation: Someone opened a second window.

Term: Provider Review

Translation: Glanced at, possibly near, your file.

Term: Account Reconsolidation

Translation: A re-confusion occurred.

Term: Miscellaneous Service

Translation: We're not telling.

Chapter 2 – The Line Item Encyclopedia

Every line item has meaning, though rarely the meaning you hope.

Item: Thermal Comfort Fee

Definition: Air was adjusted to a state approximating comfort.

Item: Supply Kit

Definition: Unnamed supplies of unspecified utility.

Item: Administrative Handling

Definition: A button was pressed with intent.

Item: Provider Convenience

Definition: Tuesday-related efficiency improvements.

Item: Assessment Package

Definition: Thinking might have occurred.

Item: Environmental Support Fee

Definition: Walls remained upright.

Item: General Usage Charge

Definition: Catch-all category for everything and nothing.

Chapter 3 – Understanding Codes

These codes form the poetic backbone of billing: structured, cryptic, and unburdened by clarity.

Code: CPT-9930X

Meaning: Something happened.

Code: CPT-0041Q

Meaning: Breathing was observed or inferred.

Code: CPT-7702R

Meaning: Routine procedures occurred non-routinely.

Code: CPT-5689C

Meaning: Equipment existed nearby.

Code: CPT-1420M

Meaning: A consult was contemplated.

Code: CPT-8009Z

Meaning: A form changed hands.

Code: CPT-9981K

Meaning: Administrative observation.

Chapter 4 – Price Determination Framework

Billing formulas represent the frontier of interpretive mathematics.

$$\text{Price} = \text{Base Cost} \times \text{Ambiguity Factor}$$

Price = Suggested Rate + (Unknown Modifier ÷ Hope)

Price = (Provider Mood × Time of Day) + Overhead

Price = Randomized Fee + Processing Lag

$$\text{Price} = (\text{Effort Estimate} \times \text{Rounding Bias})$$

$$\text{Price} = \text{Legacy Charge} \times \text{Confusion Index}$$

$$\text{Price} = \text{Variable} + \text{Variable}^2$$

Chapter 5 – Your Portion

Your responsibility expands to fill all available financial space.

Your Portion: More than expected.

Your Portion: Determined post-hope.

Your Portion: The part insurance admired but did not cover.

Your Portion: Rounded up for clarity.

Your Portion: A generous remainder.

Your Portion: Statistically higher than necessary.

Your Portion: Final amount pending further increases.

Chapter 6 – Insurance Interpretation Guide

Insurance language thrives in the gray zone between maybe and no.

"Not covered."

Meaning: We don't want to.

"Partially covered."

Meaning: You will still pay most of it.

"Reviewed."

Meaning: Looked in the direction of your claim.

"Denied."

Meaning: Because yes.

"Pending."

Meaning: Waiting for alignment of administrative planets.

"Revised."

Meaning: No improvement.

"Explained."

Meaning: Good luck.

Chapter 7 – Common Billing Questions

Common billing questions receive uncommon clarity.

Q: Why does this room cost $4,870 per night?

A: It contains walls.

Q: Why is this test $1,537?

A: It was Tuesday.

Q: Who sets these prices?

A: Committees of unknown composition.

Q: Why is this item on my bill?

A: Tradition.

Q: What does “adjusted” mean?

A: Something happened somewhere.

Q: Why is there a processing fee?

A: A file briefly moved.

Q: Can I get a breakdown?

A: No.

Chapter 8 – Diagrams & Visual Aids

Visual aids offer no additional clarity.

Diagram: Flow of Charges

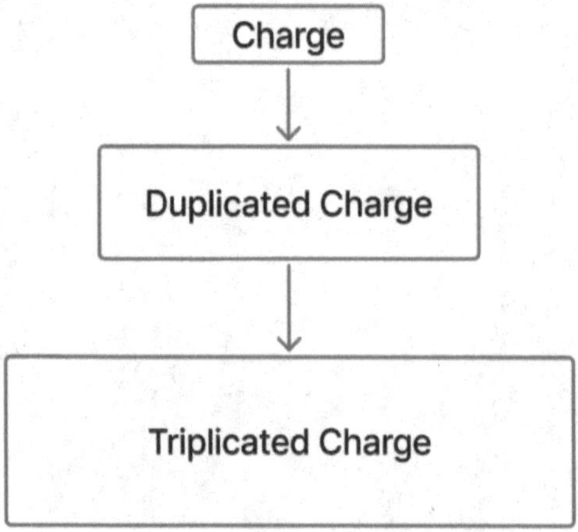

Diagram: Billing Loop

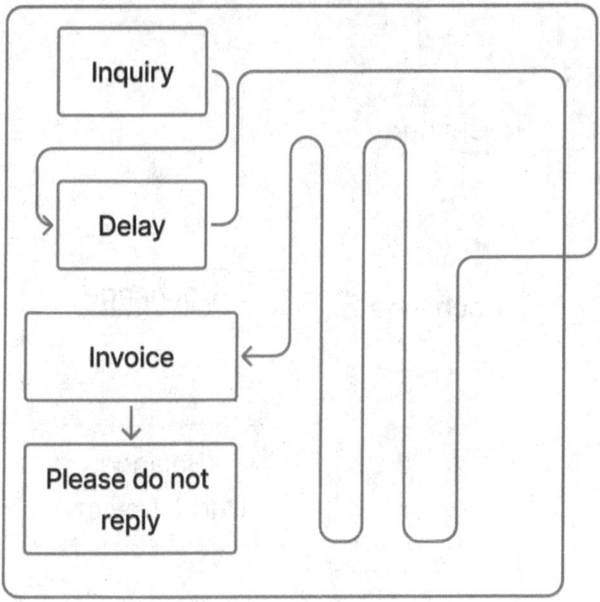

Diagram: Adjustment Spiral

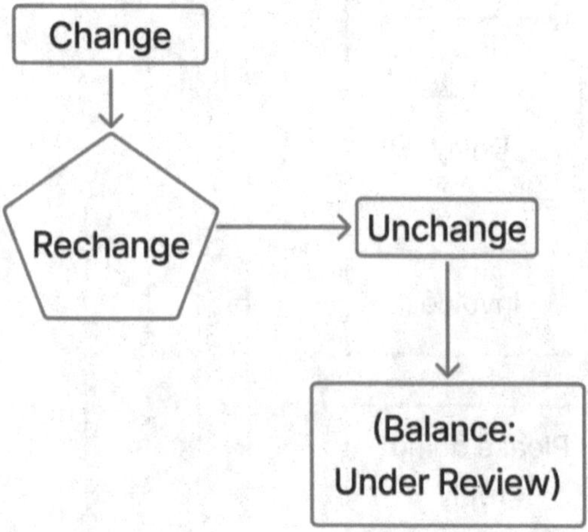

Diagram: Percentage of Responsibility

Diagram: Cost Inflation Path

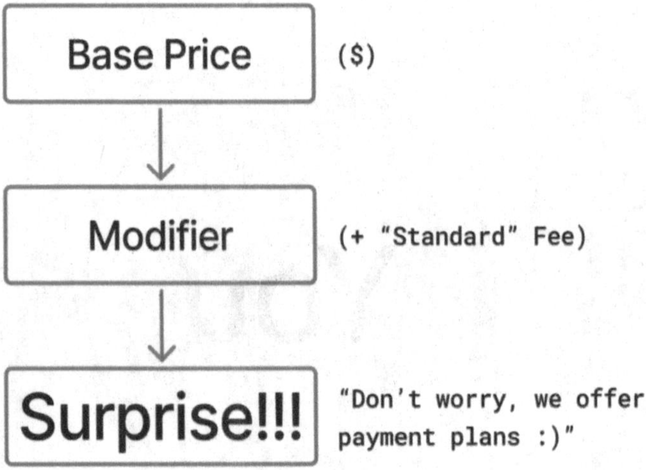

Diagram: Administrative Cycle

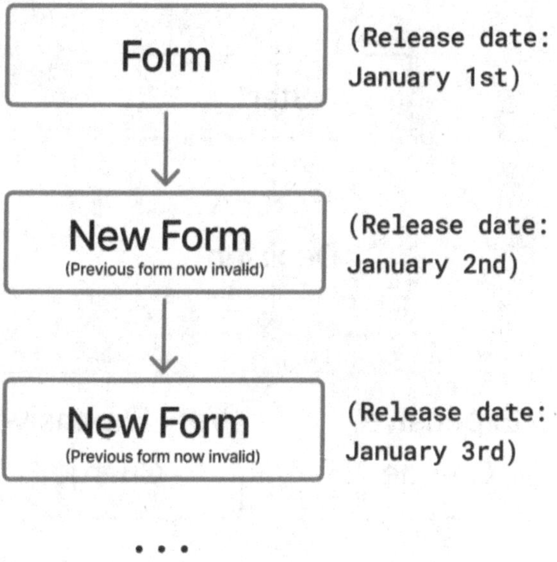

Diagram: Billing Decision Tree

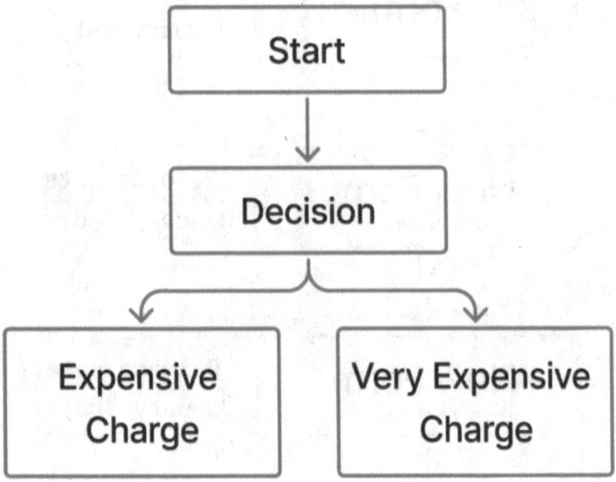

Chapter 9 – Case Studies in Confusion

Each case study is fictional, though not implausible.

Emily received a $7,921 charge for "Comprehensive Interaction."

She recalls nodding once.

Mark was billed $412 for "Ambient Services."

The room contained air.

Priya's invoice included a $566 "Equipment Presence Fee."

A cart passed by.

Dan disputed a $993 "Document Review."

The document was unopened.

Lila found a $1,202 "Processing Adjustment."

A window was minimized.

Omar paid $348 for "General Support Services."

A chair existed.

June’s bill included a $289 “Clerical Event.”

Someone walked by with a clipboard.

Chapter 10 – Glossary of Indeterminate Terms

Definitions illuminate nothing.

Term: Adjustment

Something was changed for unknown reasons.

Term: Processing

A button was pressed.

Term: Review

Looked at or near the document.

Term: Assessment

Thinking occurred, or didn't.

Term: Reconciliation

Confusion was restated.

Term: Evaluation

A decision was suggested.

Term: Processing Lag

Time moved forward.

Chapter 11 – Tables You Cannot Interpret

Tables present information without meaning.

Table: Cost Overview

Columns: Charge A | Charge B | Charge C

Table: Billing Summary

Values: 12.4 | TBD | —

Table: Modifier Map

Inputs produce outputs inconsistently.

Table: Adjustment Log

All entries adjusted.

Table: Responsibility Grid

You in all cells.

Table: Variance Index

Numbers fluctuate without cause.

Table: Fee Consolidation

All fees consolidated upward.

Chapter 12 – The Final Translation

Final translations remain as variable as the charges themselves.

“This charge may vary.”

"Interpretation pending."

"Calculation ongoing."

"Amount subject to drift."

"Cost reflective of unknown factors."

"Final total not final."

"Understanding may not occur."

About the Author

Jordan K. Ledger, M.B.A., is recognized internationally for his pioneering work in reducing clarity across corporate documents. He holds advanced credentials in PowerPoint throughput, spreadsheet inflation, and general administrative opacity. His work has been described as "comprehensively unhelpful" by several committees of unknown composition.

Acknowledgements

Appreciation to billing departments nationwide, whose tireless commitment to ambiguity has provided decades of inspiration. Any errors in this book should be considered enhancements.

Final Notes

This page is for notes that, like the Appendix pages on a PowerPoint, will never be read by anyone, ever.

"Charges remain subject to reinterpretation."

"Amounts fluctuate independently of logic."

“Billing consistent with inconsistent standards.”

“Review in progress indefinitely.”

"Pending clarification without timeline."

“Adjustment may reflect non-events.”

"Responsibility may expand."

"Documentation may increase spontaneously."

"Cost structures remain unmapped."

"Calculations may reset."

"Interpretation remains limited."

"Charges exist, therefore billed."

“Administrative cycles renew themselves.”

"Totals drift toward completion."

Next in the Ledger Series: A Beginner's Guide to Understanding Your Medical Bill.

Every page is blank.

www.ingramcontent.com/pod-product-compliance
Lightning Source LLC
LaVergne TN
LVHW040515210926
848480LV00005BA/1473

* 9 7 9 8 2 9 5 4 3 3 6 9 6 *